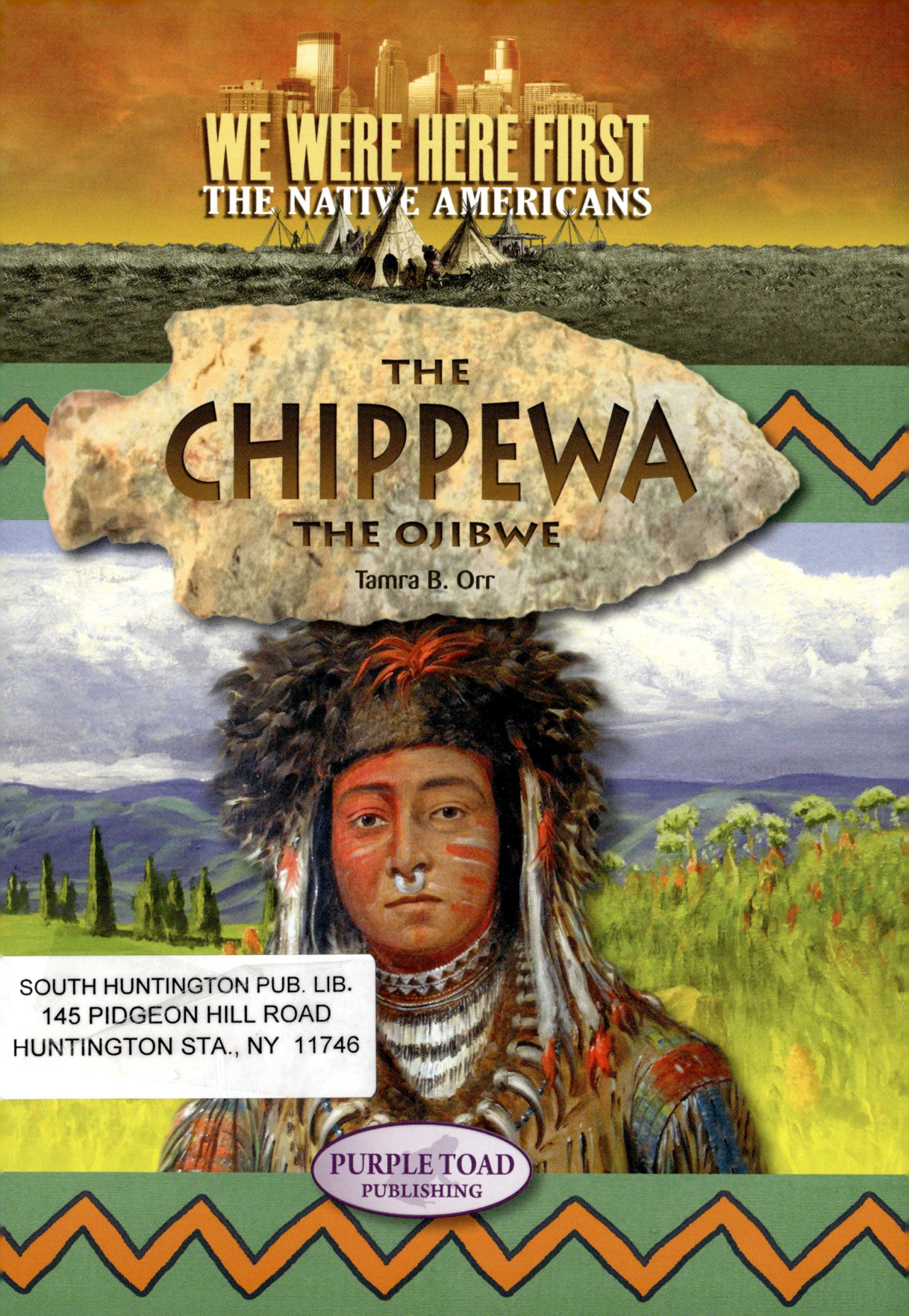

We Were Here First: The Native Americans

The Apache of the Southwest
The Blackfeet
The Cherokee
The Cheyenne
The Chippewa (The Ojibwe)
The Choctaw
The Comanche
The Creek
The Hopi
The Inuit of the Arctic
The Iroquois of the Northeast
The Lenape
The Navajo
The Nez Perce of the Pacific Northwest
The Pueblo
The Seminole
The Shawnee
The Shoshone
The Sioux of the Great Northern Plains
The Zuni

Copyright © 2020 by Purple Toad Publishing, Inc.

All rights reserved. No part of this book may be reproduced without written permission from the publisher. Printed and bound in the United States of America.

Printing 1 2 3 4 5 6 7 8 9

Library of Congress Cataloging-in-Publication Data
  Orr, Tamra B.
    The Chippewa, or Ojibwe / Written by: Tamra B. Orr
p. cm.
Includes bibliographical references, glossary, and index.
ISBN 9781624694554
  1. Chippewa (or Ojibwe)—Juvenile literature.
  2. Native American History—United States—Juvenile literature. I. Series: We Were Here First: The Chippewa
  E99. C6 2019
  997.00497
Library of Congress Control Number: 2019942435

eBook ISBN: 9781624694547

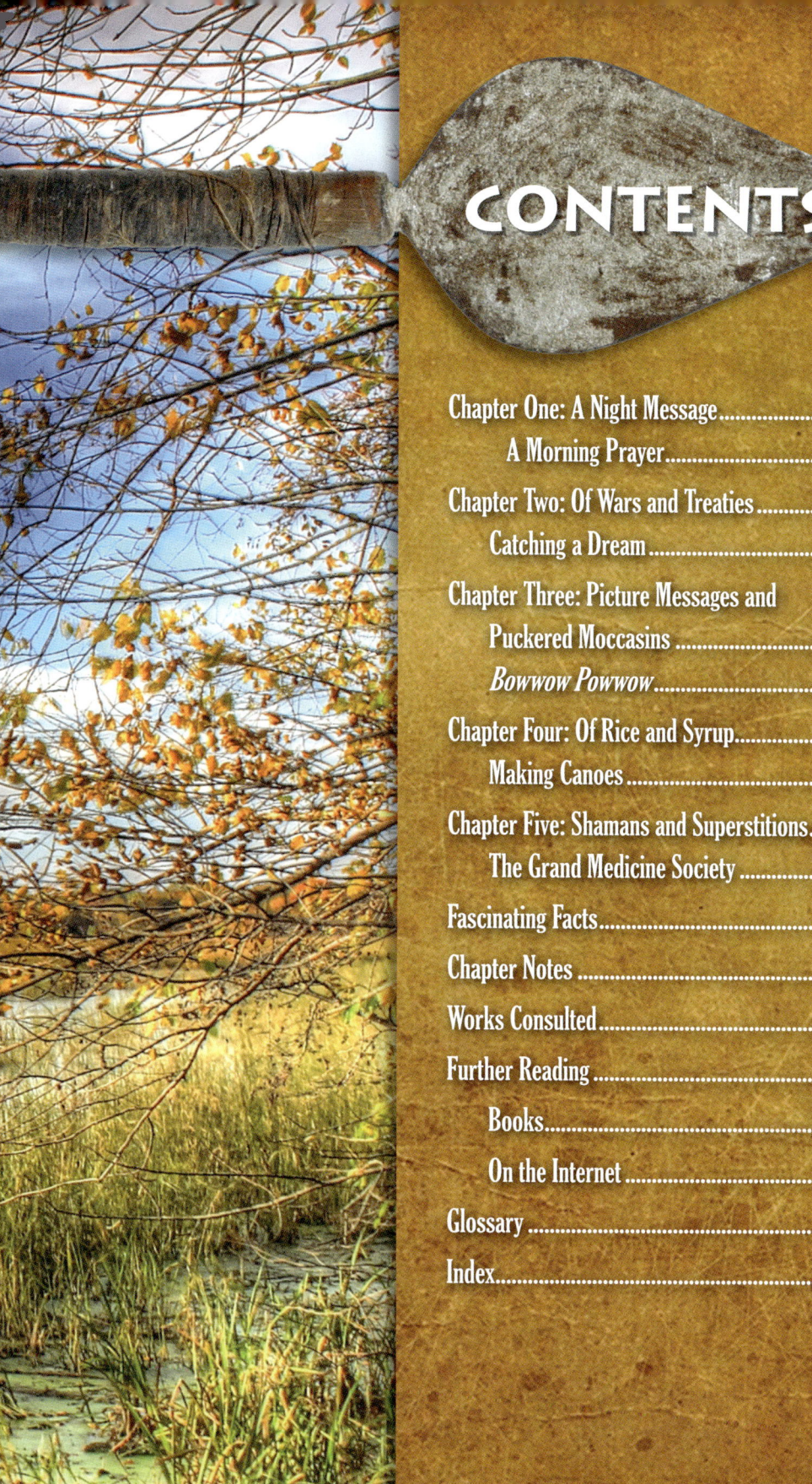

CONTENTS

Chapter One: A Night Message 5
    A Morning Prayer 11
Chapter Two: Of Wars and Treaties 13
    Catching a Dream 19
Chapter Three: Picture Messages and
    Puckered Moccasins 21
    Bowwow Powwow 27
Chapter Four: Of Rice and Syrup 29
    Making Canoes 35
Chapter Five: Shamans and Superstitions .. 37
    The Grand Medicine Society 43
Fascinating Facts 44
Chapter Notes 45
Works Consulted 45
Further Reading 46
    Books 46
    On the Internet 46
Glossary 46
Index 47

Ojibwe wigwams sheltered people from the rain and wind, and even protected them against the cold.

CHAPTER 1
A Night Message

The boy turned on his side on his woven mat and felt himself falling asleep. It was a dark and quiet night. A light breeze rippled through the trees. The murmur of the adults' voices was carried on the wind. The fire that would burn all night long crackled and snapped. He knew all of these sounds as well as he knew the trails from the village to the forest.

Suddenly, the night was interrupted by something else—a night message from one of the village's grandfathers.

"The hunting party will leave at morning light," he softly announced from outside the wigwam. "We will be searching for buffalo and return in several days." He paused, and the boy knew what was coming next. "Today, a little boy shouted at his father," the grandfather said gently. "Shouting is not allowed. We cannot have little ones making loud noises to scare away game or let our enemies know where we are. This boy must remember our rules."

Now he was wide awake. He knew the grandfather's night message was meant for him. He had yelled at Father today when Father had told him he was not yet old enough to go on

Chapter 1

Babies were often carried on mothers' backs on cradleboards in order to keep them safe and prevent them from crying.

the buffalo hunt. He knew better. He had been taught, from as long as he could remember, that children were not allowed to shout at their elders. They were to be quiet and self-controlled at all times. Even babies were not to cry, for it could one day give away the tribe's position if they were hiding from enemies or evil spirits. After he had yelled, his mother had said nothing. Instead, she rubbed charcoal dust on her hands and patted his cheeks firmly. All day long, everyone in the village who saw him knew he had done something wrong. It was shameful.

All of the girls and boys knew the tribal rules even better than they knew the surrounding trails. Children were not to shout or yell, of course, but there was much more to remember. They were never to walk between an elder and the village fire. They were forbidden from interrupting an elder. That would show disrespect. They could not laugh out loud if something unexpected happened. They also could not look wistfully or longingly at other members' food.

Sitting up, the boy closed his eyes and said a prayer to the Great Spirit for forgiveness. He knew he would remember this night message and never make the same mistake again.

Growing Up Chippewa

From the time they are babies, the Chippewa, also known as the Ojibwe or the Anishinaabeg, are taught to be quiet and obey their elders and the

A Night Message

village rules. This did not mean they did not play—they ran, laughed, and played games like other children. Many of these games were created in order to teach them skills they would need as adults. For example, girls played with birch bark dolls, learning how to sew and cook by making clothes and preparing food for them. Boys were given small bows and arrows to play with, learning how to aim and hit targets for when they would become hunters. Both boys and girls spent time learning the skill of removing bark from the birch tree, and hunting for medicinal roots.

Native Americans knew to watch for the white blossoms of the snakeroot plant.

John Rogers, or *Way-quah-gezhig*, as he was known within his tribe, remembers learning to dig for a plant called snakeroot, which would be traded as medicine. In his book *Red World and White: Memories of a Chippewa Boyhood*, he writes about how his mother taught him and his brother the process.

" . . . we stopped at a place where Mother said the gathering would be best. Here we took our hoes and sacks from the wagon and waited for further instructions. 'Here,' said mother, 'is one of the roots. Look at it. See how it grows. Notice the shapes of the leaves. They are long and pointed, something like the grass that grows by the lakes. To dig for them you hit down with your hoe, then give a little jerk. Next, grab the grass and pull. You will find that it is much like an octopus. Now hit the roots against the hoe and the dirt will fall away. Break off the green tops and put the roots in your sack.' Soon my brother and I were bragging over our speed in pulling the snakeroot. It was a contest as to who would get the biggest root for his sack."[1]

Chapter 1

The Chippewa hunted the large buffalo, or bison, for meat, as well as for offerings for their guardian spirits.

When children reached puberty, their lives began to change to prepare them for adulthood. Boys were expected to go through a vision quest. First, they spent up to four days completely alone, praying and fasting, drinking only water. Then, during their dreams, they were expected to find their guardian spirit. This spirit would be with them through the rest of their lives, protecting and guiding them. In return, the Chippewa would offer their guardians gifts such as food and tobacco. After girls reached puberty, they were also kept alone for several days. Although they were not expected to go through a vision quest, if a girl had a vision while she was alone, she was considered to be specially blessed.

Most Chippewa children, as well as adults, did not have actual names. Instead they were simply known as whatever role they played within the

A Night Message

tribe. Older men and women were called Grandfather and Grandmother. Parents were all Mother and Father. Children were often just referred to as "number two boy" or "number four girl." Brothers and sisters typically called each other *nii-she-may* for a younger sibling or *nii-sa-yay* for an older one.

On the other hand, Chippewa families were known as clans. They were named after animals or birds. Each of the clans had a specific responsibility. One clan, for example, might act as the chiefs of the village, helping to set rules and solve problems. They were frequently named after birds, such as loons or cranes. Another clan might be the teachers, in charge of sharing skills and information with children. Other clans were given the job of healers, hunters, gatherers, or spiritual leaders. Warrior clans were often named after fierce animals such as the bear or wolf.

The Chippewa is one of the largest native tribes in North America. They lived throughout the Great Lakes area of Minnesota, Wisconsin, North Dakota, and Michigan, as well as

Chippewa families often just referred to each other by what role they played within the family.

Chapter 1

The Chippewa tribe spread throughout both the northern United States and into Canada.

parts of southern Canada. Over time, they moved into Iowa and Missouri and into the Great Plains. Today, about 150 different groups live on reservations in the United States and Canada. Each reservation has its own government, school systems, law enforcement, and leaders—much like small or independent countries.

A Morning Prayer

This traditional Chippewa morning prayer shows the tribe's connection to and appreciation for the beauty of nature. It also demonstrates their belief in a greater power (The Great Spirit) and how they picture their place or role in the world.

Oh Great Spirit, whose voices I hear in the winds
And whose breath gives life to everyone,
Hear me.
I come to you as one of your many children;
I am weak . . . I am small . . . I need your wisdom and strength.
Let me walk in beauty, and make my eyes ever
Behold the red and purple sunsets.
Make my hands respect the things you have made,
And make my ears sharp so I may hear your voice.
Make me wise, so that I may understand what you
Have taught my people and
The lessons you have hidden in each leaf and each rock.
I ask for wisdom and strength,
Not to be superior to my brothers, but to be able
To fight my greatest enemy, myself.
Make me ever ready to come before you with
Clean hands and a straight eye,
So as life fades away as a fading sunset,
My spirit may come to you without shame.[2]

Young Chippewa girls often spent time making baskets and sewing clothes with their friends.

European explorers claimed many parts of the United States for their home countries, creating territorial battles for ownership.

Chapter 2
Of Wars and Treaties

Life had been fairly simple for the Chippewa until the arrival of the Europeans in the early 17th century. Since 100 C.E., the tribe had lived in the northern Upper Peninsula of the Great Lakes region. They were excellent fishermen, catching walleye, whitefish, sturgeon, and suckers with their nets, traps, and fishing poles during the summer months. In the spring, they turned to spearfishing, and in the winter, they were ice fishing. More than 100,000 Chippewa lived throughout the region. They often moved from one place to another to stay close to the most plentiful food sources.

Everything changed when European explorers came to the area. France claimed the land for New France. The French bonded with the Chippewa to fight against the invading British, as well as any anti-French tribes. French fur traders from Canada began trading with the Chippewa. The Europeans brought all new weapons, including knives and guns, to the tribe. This gave the Chippewa the ability to have more power to protect their lands.

At War

The next century brought a stream of new wars. In the French and Iroquois Wars (1640–1701), the Iroquois tribes fought

Chapter 2

Like with many Native American tribes, the Chippewa depended greatly on squash and corn for food.

against the French and their allies, including the Chippewa. During the French and Indian Wars (1688–1763), Queen Anne's War (1702–1713), and the First French Fox War (1712–1716), the Chippewa continued to side with the French against other tribes and the British. During these years, the tribe continued to expand. They established a large village on Madeline Island at the mouth of Chequamegon Bay. There, they planted corn and squash, grew wild rice, and spent hours fishing and hunting. Each summer, Chippewa members came from across the region to visit the island for religious celebrations. Some Chippewa moved into Lower Michigan and southern Ontario. As trade increased and battles were won, they slowly expanded into the Great Plains.

In 1763, the ongoing conflict between the French and the English finally came to an end, with England the winner. Much of the Chippewa's land was claimed for Britain and its colonies. During the Revolutionary War (1775–1783), however, the Chippewa joined forces with the British in order to fight the American colonists. In 1785, the Chippewa merged with other tribes to form the Western Confederacy. Their common goal was to keep the Ohio River as the boundary between their tribal lands and U.S. settlements. They

In this painting, artist John Trumbull captures the moment of General Montgomery's death during the attack on Quebec.

Chapter 2

failed, and by the time the U.S. had claimed much of the land, the Chippewa found themselves forced off their lands and onto reservations.

A Time of Treaties

Once the United States gained control of most of their land, the Chippewa, like many other Native American tribes, had little choice but to move. Since much of their land was rich in

Chunks of copper like this one (above) made Native American land valuable and sought after by settlers. Items made by Native Americans using copper include a copper knife, spearpoints, awls, and a spade (right).

Of Wars and Treaties

Log cabins provided the Chippewa with sturdier homes, with far more protection from cold, wind, and rain.

valuable copper and timber, settlers were eager to claim it. Before and after the Indian Removal Act of 1830, a number of treaties were written and signed, and the Chippewa began to move. Many of the reservations they were sent to were far too small to fit everyone. From 1854 to 1856, the tribe was shuffled to reservations, making life for these Native Americans very difficult.

By the 1880s, life again changed drastically for the Chippewa people. Their traditional homes had been replaced with log cabins or tarpaper shacks. The wigwams that still existed were made with blankets instead of

Chapter 2

Birch bark canoes were sturdy yet light. They were fast and easy to maneuver.

animal skins, and cardboard instead of woven matting. By the 1940s, only the oldest generation still spoke the original language, and few wore traditional clothing. Canoes, once made of birch bark, were now made of wood or metal.

In recent years, there has been a push to bring back Native American traditions, including with the Chippewa. They are once again teaching their original language to schoolchildren, returning to making tribal arts and crafts, and honoring their history through story and song.

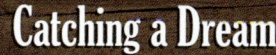

Catching a Dream

Dream catchers are now used by people of many different cultures as art or decoration.

The Chippewa strongly believed that important messages from the gods and spirits were sent to people through their dreams. Good dreams were usually visions from good spirits and were welcomed. Nightmares, or bad dreams, on the other hand, were from bad spirits and feared. To help ensure babies and small children had only good dreams, the tribe's women often made dream catchers to hang over the child's cradleboard or bed.

Dream catchers were made with a loop of thin willow branch formed in a circle or teardrop shape. Sinew was woven into a spiderweb pattern in the middle to honor the god Asibikaashi, the legendary Spider Woman who watched over young children. It was usually decorated with feathers, to represent air. Owl feathers were used for girls and eagle feathers for boys. Sometimes stone or bone beads were added.

These handmade charms were thought to be able to catch good dreams and hold on to them, while bad dreams would drift through the holes in the web and be blown away. Over time, the dream catchers would begin to fall apart, but that was all right with the Chippewa. To them, it was a symbol that a child was growing into adulthood.

While many different Native American tribes have made dream catchers, it is the Chippewa who are credited with making the very first ones. Want to make your own dream catcher? There are many fun projects with directions online, including one at http://www.nativetech.org/dreamcat/dreminst.html.

This thunderbird image is considered one of the main crests of the Chippewa people.

Chapter 3
Picture Messages and Puckered Moccasins

Without a written language, how can you pass on an important message to someone? If you were a Chippewa, you used picture messages. By drawing familiar images on rocks, hides, or bones, you could say anything from "I will meet you at the hunting grounds at sunset" to "Beware! There is danger nearby." The Chippewa often used these symbols to tell stories.

For example, this symbol could mean, "Bear alive."

On the other hand, this one could mean, "Bear dead."[1]

What do you think these symbols might mean? (campfire)

(camp)

From Symbols to the Alphabet

One look at a few words in Chippewa and you will notice something very different from English. The Chippewa use a lot of vowels—especially *a*. Their alphabet is made up of these letters: a, aa, b, ch, d, e, g, h, ', i, ii, j, k, m, n, o, oo, p, s, sh, t, w, y, z, zh.

Chapter 3

Here are a few examples of Chippewa words: [2]

emikwaan	spoon
anishinaabe	person
oodena	town
niin	I
aaniin	Hello
miigwech	thank you
jiimaanens	small boat
agaashiinyi	someone is small
gaawiin ingikendanziin	I don't know it

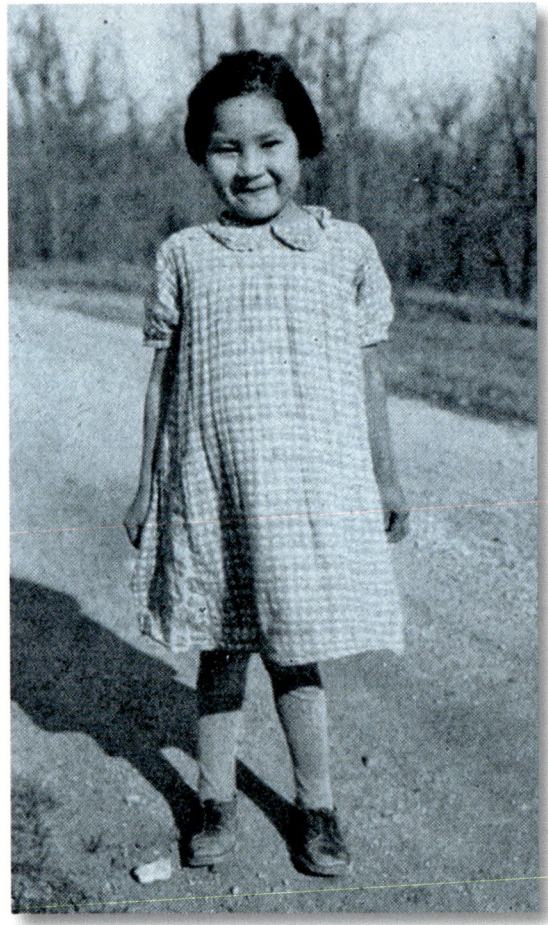

The Chippewa language, often referred to as Anishinaabemowin, is considered to be almost extinct today, but people are trying to change that. Schools in states such as Montana and Michigan are offering programs that teach the language to young children. Finding teachers has been tough—most of the native speakers are elderly. "People in their 80s don't want to come and teach school, especially dealing with three, four, or five-year-olds," says Gerald Gray Sr., language program director in Great Falls, Montana.

Chippewa children like this girl in 1938 did not have access to schools that would teach their native language.

One Chippewa member named Standing Rock agreed to help. He knew that otherwise, his native language might be lost forever. "There's still quite a few [native speakers] out there, but they're like us; they're gradually drifting away, like the cloud." More than 400 children have gone through the learning program so far. "By doing what they're doing here, I believe we'll survive," said Standing Rock.[3]

From Head to Toe

Because the Chippewa lived outside year round, the clothes they wore had to keep them warm—or cool—and dry. They also had to rely on whatever materials they had nearby. For many tribes, including the Chippewa, these materials were leather, furs, and feathers. Some plant materials were woven to make softer garments. Chippewa men usually wore leather breechcloths and leggings in the summer. In the winter, they added long tops called tunics, as well as long robes or cloaks. Women wore deerskin dresses and wraparound skirts. Under these skirts they sometimes wore petticoats made out of woven nettles or thistles.

The people decorated their clothing with brightly colored plant-based dyes, as well as with beads made from shells, coral, turquoise, copper, silver, wood, amber, ivory, or animal horns or bones. Wearing feathers was a sign of bravery and honor. Jewelry was often added as well.

Adding colorful beads to clothing was one way that the Chippewa made their clothes special.

Chapter 3

A necklace made with antler tips and silver beads in-between.

Necklaces were made of animal claws or teeth. Later, after the Europeans came, glass beads decorated all types of clothing.

When many people think of Native Americans, they picture them all wearing moccasins. While it is true that virtually all tribes wore these leather shoes, the styles and shapes were different from one tribe to the next. All were made out of tanned leather and sewn together. However, some groups

Picture Messages and Puckered Moccasins

added beads, while others added quills. Some painted designs on the shoes, and others trimmed them with animal fur.

The Chippewa made puckered moccasins suited for easy travel over the leaves and pine needles that covered the forest floor. The word *Ojibwe*, which is another name for the Chippewa, means "people of the puckered moccasin." These shoes were made of three pieces of leather: the sole, the upper shoe, and the tongue. Women used bone or thorn needles to sew the pieces together. Thread was either sinew or spun from plant fibers. Tough moose hide was often used for the sole. The upper shoe, which wrapped around the ankle, was soft deerskin. The tongue was usually made from caribou and decorated with embroidered, colorful flowers or a piece of velvet. The seam around the toes pulled the leather, making it pucker. There were no right and left moccasins—they were the same.

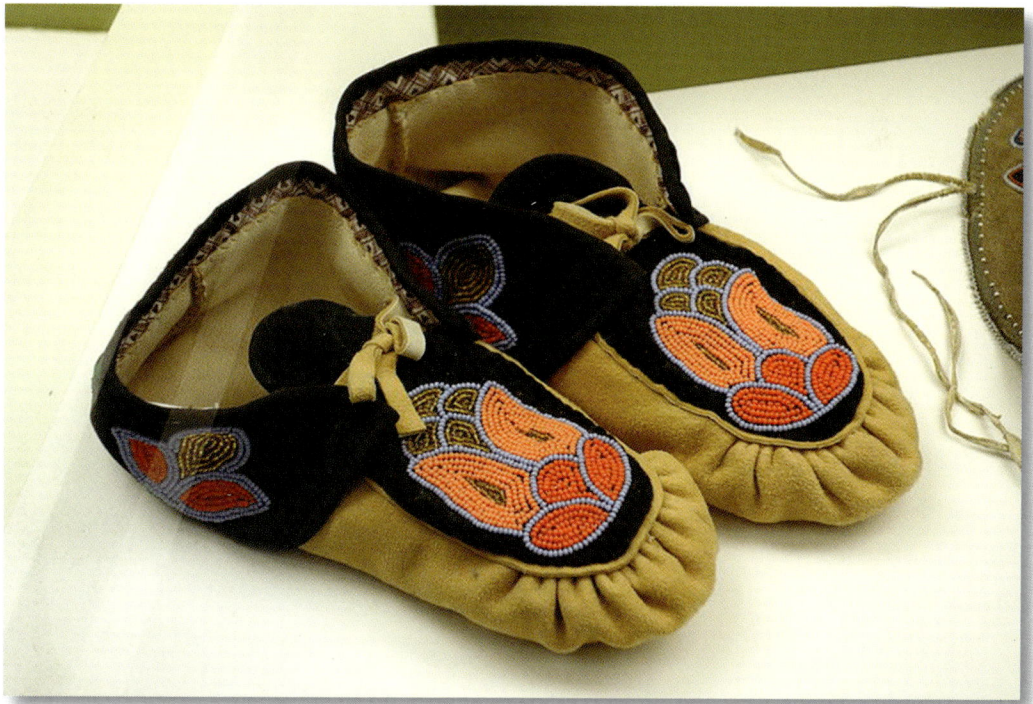

Moccasins varied greatly from one Native American tribe to another, both in style and how they were decorated. These puckered moccasins were worn by the Chippewa. The leather was decorated with many tiny glass beads.

Chapter 3

The clothing of the Chippewa men was often more decorated and embroidered than the women's clothing.

Both men and women tended to wear their hair long, often in braids. During times of war, some of the men would shave their heads, leaving only one long lock of hair in the center. They likely believed that this scalp lock made them look fiercer.

Bowwow Powwow

For years, University of Minnesota professor Brenda Child had researched and written books about Native American history, but soon she had a new idea. She wanted to share what she had learned about the Chippewa powwow celebrations with children. She also wanted to honor the language of the tribe. In 2018, she published *Bowwow Powwow*, a picture book about the traditional dance—and dogs.

Bowwow Powwow focuses on Windy Girl, a young Chippewa girl. She is attending a powwow with her uncle and her dog, Itchy Boy. While there, she has a dream about dogs dancing in full Native American clothing. Child's book has something else unique—it is written in English and in Ojibwe. An Illinois teacher translated her words, and a local artist did the illustrations.

"One night, Windy had a weird and wonderful dream about a special powwow," reads one page. It is followed by the Native American translation, "*Aabiding depikadinig, gaa-izhi-bawaadang niimi'idiwin Noodinikwens. Gii-maamakaadaabandam.*"

Child was born on the Red Lake Indian Reservation in Illinois and spent many years there, so helping readers learn about Native American language is important to her. "I . . . wanted it to be a bilingual children's book to help language educators and families," she says. "But some of the purpose of doing a children's book is just to have fun."[4]

Many Chippewa families had a dog as both a family pet and to help with hunting.

Wild turkeys were a main part of the Chippewa diet if they lived near the Great Plains.

CHAPTER 4
OF RICE AND SYRUP

For the Chippewa, meal choices largely depended on where they lived and what time of year it was. If the group lived close to the Great Lakes, they ate lots of fish and other water creatures, such as crayfish, mussels, frogs, and turtles. If the forest was closer than the water, food was more likely some type of game, such as squirrel, deer, raccoon, bear, or beaver. In the Great Plains, it might also include buffalo or wild turkey. Hunters relied on bows and arrows most of the time, but they also used hatchets, spears, lances, and knives. After the Europeans came, many hunters used guns for hunting as well. Everyone in the tribe learned how to dig for roots and gather wild vegetables. They also planted crops of squash, corn, beans, and pumpkin.

Wild mushrooms were a popular choice to add to a dish, along with cattail roots and wild onions. During the summer months, everyone picked grapes, hazelnuts, and every kind of non-poisonous berry. Without a way to keep the food cold, the Chippewa either ate the fruit or found a way to preserve it. Often they would take berries and lay them on rocks to dry in the sun. The dried fruit was then put in deep, underground pits so that wild animals could not steal it.

Chapter 4

Campfires were a key to survival during the winter months. They provided heat, helped cook food, and kept animals away.

As the seasons changed, so did the daily lives of the Chippewa. During the cold winter months, they endured—hoping to find enough to eat to survive another year. They relied on the dried fruit and maple syrup and rice they had put aside during the summer. They lived in isolation during the coldest months, trapping and hunting. Stories were told around campfires. Women sewed new clothes. Games and music were played to pass the snowy days. Children went sledding on toboggans and put snowshoes on their feet to walk into the forests.

Each family had its own wigwam, or home. Some of these homes were dome-shaped, while others were rectangular or cone-shaped. They had wooden frames that were covered in layers of birch bark or animal hides. Most of them were usually between 8 and 10 feet tall and 10 to 15 feet wide. A hole was left in the wall for a door, and one was in the ceiling to let

Of Rice and Syrup

smoke from cooking fires escape. Tribes in the Plains tended to build tepees instead of wigwams. These homes were made of hides wrapped around a triangle of long wooden poles. Both wigwams and tepees were fast to build (often taking less than a full day) and even faster to take apart and move when needed.

Once spring arrived, it was time to move on. Families packed up and moved into large villages of hundreds of people. It was a chance to see friends and family, share food, and enjoy the return of the sun.

Teepees were simple structures that were best in the spring and summer months.

Chapter 4

Manoominike-giizis, the Ricing Moon

In autumn, as the weather turned colder, the Chippewa watched for the "ricing moon." When they saw it, they knew it was time to harvest the wild rice that had been growing for months. It was a difficult, slow process but it kept the tribe fed during the winter months when game was much harder to find.

Ricing was hard work. Using a long pole called a *gahndakeeigunahk*, men and women pushed a canoe through thick reeds. These reeds grew as tall as 12 feet. As the men slowly moved the canoe through the water, women reached out with *bahwaigunahkoog*, or two long sticks. Using these sticks, they bent the reeds into the boat and then hit the heads, causing ripe rice grains to fall into the bottom of the canoe. Some grains fell into the water to re-seed for the next year. Depending on the size of the rice field, it could take a few hours to an entire day to fill a canoe. Since the rice was still growing, it was common to go out several times throughout the month to gather more of the grain.

Ricing canoes were used for long hours during the rice harvest.

Of Rice and Syrup

Collecting the sap from maple trees took work, but the syrup helped the tribes get though long winters.

After the rice was harvested, there was still more work to do. It had to be slowly dried and roasted over a fire. After that, it was pounded with long-handled poles or stomped on for hours with strong feet. This removed the hull, or outer covering of the grain. Finally the rice was ready to be used in flour, added to soups, or boiled by itself.

Sweet Sap

Just as the Chippewa watched carefully for the ricing moon, they also listened carefully for the return of the crows in the spring. Not only did this sound mean that the tribe had survived another winter, but also that it was almost time to pack up and head for the maple syrup camp.

Much of the land where the Chippewa lived had thick forests. In these forests were maple trees—the trees that produce the sap that is used to make maple syrup. In early spring, as the the sap began to run, Chippewa

Chapter 4

Nettle stems contained strong linen-like fibers and were quite strong. They were used to make fishing nets.

families would move into the forests to tap the trees. Each year, they would return to the same spot and set up a temporary house.

Once they tapped the maple trees, they hung buckets on the trunks to catch the sap. It took about 40 gallons of sap to make a single gallon of syrup, so the process took time. While they waited for buckets to fill, the Chippewa frequently wove fishing nets and removed the bark from birch trees. Weaving a fishing net from nettles took hundreds of hours, and kept the people busy.

Once the buckets were full, they were poured into *mokoks*, vessels made from birch bark. These were carried back to camp full of syrup, which had to be boiled, or buried in the woods until the sap was needed. Maple syrup was used in many ways. After it was boiled down for many hours, it was added to food to sweeten it, or left to harden into candy.

Making Canoes

The Chippewa made the most of what they could find in nature, and this was especially true with the birch tree. Its wood was used for lumber, but its thin, paper-like bark had many uses. It was used to cover the wooden frames of their homes. It was used to wrap the bodies of the dead before burial. It was also used to make torches and to cover the wooden frames of toboggans and canoes.

Canoes were a vital part of Chippewa life. They were used for fishing and for transporting goods to sell and trade. They were also used in races for fun.

Canoes were typically made of strong, lightweight wood. The ribs were usually strong pieces of hickory, cut into long strips and bent to the shape of the canoe. The wooden frames were covered with birch bark. Seams were sealed with pine or spruce gum. Paddles were carved from birch or other types of wood.

Most of the canoes measured 22 feet long and 3 feet wide. They could carry four or five people, plus cargo. These lightweight boats were easy to steer in all kinds of water, from fast-running rivers to shallow marshland. This made them perfect for long hours of fishing or ricing, traveling to a trading post along the river, or rushing off to take part in battle.

Canoes were a part of daily life for those tribes living near the water. Like today's cars, they moved people from place to place to trade or visit.

In this painting by Joseph Henry Sharp, a chief is buried with his possessions about him to bring to the afterlife. Various herbs and medicine are hung to ward off evil spirits.

CHAPTER 5
SHAMANS AND SUPERSTITIONS

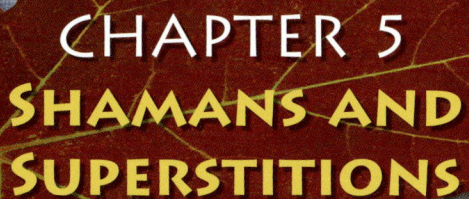

The Chippewa world was full of spiritual beings and ghosts. Some of them were there to guide and protect Chippewa. The sun and moon were spirits that helped people. Thunder and lightning brought rain and filled the sky with wonder. The Great Spirit, Kiccimanito, watched over them all, making sure they stayed healthy, found game in the forest and fish in the lakes, and were the victors in battles.

But ghosts and witches also surrounded the Chippewa, and they were frequently angry and looking for vengeance. Many of the tribe referred to their land as "haunted hunting grounds," as they believed the acres were full of the ghosts of those who had lived there before. They were on the edges of streams. They were in the trees. If one of the Chippewa sensed one of these hostile spirits nearby, it was time to run.

Truman Fox, in an article written for Michigan State University's College of Social Science, described what happened when a tribal member thought a ghost had come to the forest during maple syrup, or sugar bushing, season. "Sometimes, during sugar-making," he stated, "they would be seized with a sudden panic, and leave everything—their kettles of sap boiling, their *mokoks* of sugar standing in their camps, and their ponies tethered in the woods—and flee helter-skelter to their canoes, as though pursued by the Evil

Chapter 5

The Chippewa believed that the eagle could carry their prayers up to the heavens.

One. In answer to the question asked in regard to the cause of their panic," he continued, "the invariable answer was a shake of the head, and a mournful *'an-do-gwane'* (don't know)." [1]

Whether or not hostile ghosts were lurking in the area—and what they would have done if they were—is unknown. Some enemy tribes of the Chippewa, however, took advantage of this belief. They hid near the villages or camps and scared the people into abandoning their homes. Then the enemy would take over the homes, land, and belongings the people left behind.

Shamans and Superstitions

An Element of Nature

Everything in a Chippewa's life was spiritual and every element of nature, including themselves, worked together to live in harmony. Animals, including birds, were respected and honored. Animals were given an important set of rights in the Chippewa world:

- Right to love and respect
- Right to protection
- Right to live a full life
- Right to grow and multiply
- Right to freedom
- Right to share fellowship
- Right to share the goodness of creation

Sacred animals included the eagle, wolf, fox, and snake. When an animal was killed or a plant was cut to provide food for the tribe, it was thanked. No one ever took more than they needed.

The People's Shamans

When children hit puberty, they went through a vision quest. Some of these young people seemed to have deeper, longer, or more profound dreams than others. They often saw future events. One Chippewa shaman described what his vision quest had been like:

"When I reached the age of puberty, my father wished me to fast, that I might become holy; invincible and invulnerable in war; become like one of those about

To the Chippewa, the wolf was like a teacher or guide to the spirit world.

Chapter 5

Shamans were well respected. They had many roles, including healing the sick in their village.

whom tales are told in the future. Thus I would be if I made special effort in my fasting. I would be 'blessed' with long life, he told me; I would be able to cure the sick; life would not be able to harm me in any way. No one would dare to be uncivil to me for fear of incurring my enmity. He pleaded with me to fast long and intently, for only then would the various spirits 'bless' me." [3]

These tribal members were then considered to be shamans, or priests. The more skilled they were, the higher the degree, or order, they reached. These people worked to keep the tribe safe and healthy. They played a vast number of roles within the group. They were doctors, pharmacists, surgeons, and psychiatrists, using their knowledge to help any member of the tribe who was injured, sick, or scared. Some shamans even helped their people fall in love. No Chippewa could marry someone in their own clan. They were willing, however, to occasionally use a medicine of herbs that might make the right person fall in love with them. [4]

Shamans and Superstitions

The Chippewa Today

In 1924, all Native Americans born in the U.S. became American citizens, including the Chippewa. By the 1940s, many of them lived on reservations throughout the United States and Canada. They were taught how to use modern farming equipment. Children went to traditional public schools. Leather clothing was replaced with American styles. Some traditions carried over, however.

The annual powwow celebrations continue today, bringing families together to dance, visit, and meet new and old friends. Traditional costumes are worn, complete with feathers, beads, and leather leggings. Songs are sung, accompanied by drums, bells, and flutes. Dancers of all ages honor their past by dancing in circles in age-old rhythms. "The pow wow is a living cultural expression of song, dance, and art which brings people together, and through the drum, reminds us of our connection to Mother Earth," wrote Harold Flett in his book, *Customs and Beliefs*. "Pow wows are a time to put differences aside and to celebrate traditions, mostly it is the time to celebrate life. A pow wow strengthens an entire race of people. To

Colorful headdresses are still part of today's powwows, which honor the Chippewa's traditions.

Chapter 5

be Anishinabe [Chippewa]," he added, "is to be proud, to know who you are, and where you came from."5

As of 2019, there were more than 100,000 Chippewa living in the same places the tribes once lived: Minnesota, Michigan, Wisconsin, Montana, and North Dakota, as well as Ontario and Saskatchewan in Canada. They are considered the third largest Native American group in the world, following the Cherokee and the Navajo. The tribal members still focus on growing and harvesting rice, while others have businesses in farming and trapping, or working in bait shops, campgrounds, fish hatcheries, and lumber stores. Thanks to the rights in their treaties and court decisions during the late 1980s, the Chippewa are allowed to hunt, fish, and harvest their rice on the same lands where their ancestors once lived.

During this pow wow in Lake Superior, Michigan, people had the chance to see the wild colors and hear the lively music of the local Chippewa.

The Grand Medicine Society

Chief Medicine Man Axel Pasey and his family at Grand Portage, Minnesota, in 1936

The Chippewa believed that good health and long life were largely due to the kindness of the gods. Their medicine men and women (and even children) were also priests, and were part of the tribe's Grand Medicine Society. Each person was trained in a specific skill. For example, some would study the different plants that could be used for healing illnesses or injuries. Others learned about the herbs that might help people have stronger or more powerful vision quests. Training might take a year—or decades.

Whatever level each priest had reached was shown in the medicine bundle he or she carried. This bundle was made out of cloth. In it were hides from different types of animals, including otter, mink, or weasel. The type of hide symbolized the level of the priest. Often other items were placed inside the medicine bundle, including shells, beads, tobacco, dried roots, herbs, or bear claws.

New priests were welcomed into the tribe during the Great Medicine Dance. Lasting anywhere from one to five days, this celebration was full of food, music, and dancing. Sacred drums and pipes were played. Songs were sung. Priests brought gifts such as blankets or wild rice. In return, the new priests were officially accepted as new tribal healers.

FASCINATING FACTS

Nation — Chippewa

Names — Chippewa are also known as Ojibwe, Ojibwa, and Anishinaabeg.

Language — Their language is a branch of the Algonquian family.

Location — The majority of the Chippewa live in Canada today.

Houses — Depending on where they lived, the Chippewa built wigwams or tepees.

Friends and enemies — The Chippewa got along well with the Potawatomi and Ottawa tribes and called themselves the Council of Three Fires. However, they often fought the Sioux and Iroquois tribes.

Crafts — Known for their use of birch bark, the Chippewa also were the first tribe to make dream catchers.

Chapter Notes

Chapter 1
1. Rogers, John. *Red World and White: Memories of a Chippewa Boyhood*. University of Oklahoma Press, 1957, pp. 11–12. Excerpted at Minnesota Indian Affairs Council and the Minnesota Humanities Center. "Why Treaties Matter." http://treatiesmatter.org/exhibit/wp-content/uploads/2017/09/Ways-of-Learning_An-Ojibwe-Childhood.pdf
2. "Ojibwa Prayer." First People. https://www.firstpeople.us/html/Ojibwa_Prayer.html

Chapter 3
1. "Native American Symbol Stories." Mr. Donn. http://nativeamericans.mrdonn.org/stories/symbols.html
2. Ojibwe People's Dictionary. "About the Ojibwe Language." https://ojibwe.lib.umn.edu/about-ojibwe-language
3. Ambarian, Jonathan. "Little Shell Tribe Works to Revitalize Language." KRTV.com November 10, 2016. http://www.krtv.com/story/33680010/little-shell-tribe-works-to-revitalize-language
4. Weber, Tom. "Miscast 'Begging Dance' Sparks Children's Book Written in Ojibwe and English.'" MPR News. June 8, 2018. https://www.mprnews.org/story/2018/06/08/brenda-child-childrens-book-powwow-ojibwe-indian-english

Chapter 5
1. "Ojibwe." University of Michigan. http://geo.msu.edu/extra/geogmich/ojibwe.html
2. Flett, Harold. "Customs and Beliefs." *Chi Ki Ken Da Mun.* April 19, 2008. https://ojibwenativeamericans.weebly.com/traditions.html
3. Copway, George. *The Traditional History and Characteristic Sketches of the Ojibway Nation*. New York: AMS Press, 1978, p.7 . Accessed at http://ojibwanation.blogspot.com/
4. William S. Lyon. *Encyclopedia of Native American Shamanism: Sacred Ceremonies of North America.* Santa Barbara, California: ABC-CLIO, 1998. Accessed at http://ojibwanation.blogspot.com/
5. Flett.

Works Consulted

Works Consulted
Alchin, Linda. "Chippewa Tribe." WarPaths2PeacePipes. https://www.warpaths2peacepipes.com/indian-tribes/chippewa-tribe.htm
"American Indian Moccasins: Ojibway, Pucker-Top and Soft-Soled Moccasion." Native American Life Living Art. http://www.snowwowl.com/naartmoccasins.html#softsole
Anishnaabeg Binaadiziwin: *An Ojibwe Peoples Resource*. http://ojibweresources.weebly.com/from-then-to-now.html
"Midewiwin: The Original Way." *Ojibwe Native Americans.* https://ojibwenativeamericans.weebly.com/religion.html
Ojibwe. Michigan State University. http://geo.msu.edu/extra/geogmich/ojibwe.html
Ojibwe Native Americans: "Traditions." https://ojibwenativeamericans.weebly.com/traditions.html
"Ojibwa Religion and Expressive Culture." *Countries and Their Cultures.* http://www.everyculture.com/North-America/Ojibwa-Religion-and-Expressive-Culture.html
Roy, Loriene. "Ojibwa." *Countries and Their Cultures.* http://www.everyculture.com/multi/Le-Pa/Ojibwa.html
Treuer, Anton. "Ojibwe Lifeways." *Minnesota Conservation Volunteer*, September–October 2012, pp. 38–46. chrome-extension://ihgdgpjankaehldoaimdlekdidkjfghe/viewer.html#https://files.dnr.state.mn.us/mcvmagazine/young_naturalists/young-naturalists-article/ojibwe/ojibwe.pdf

Further Reading

Books

Diemer-Eaton, Jessica. *A Day at the Sugar Camp.* Evansville, Indiana: Woodland Indian Educational Programs, 2014.

Halvorson, Alesha. *The Ojibwe (American Indian Life).* North Mankato, Minnesota: Capstone Press, 2018.

Lowden, Stephanie Golightly. *Time of the Eagle*: A Story of an Ojibwe Winter. Minneapolis, Minnesota: Midwest Traditions, 2006.

Minnesota Historical Society. *Ojibwe Shoulder Bag Kit.* St. Paul, Minnesota: Minnesota Historical Society Press, 2013.

Ramsey, Torren. *Ojibwe (Spotlight on Native Americans).* York, Pennsylvania: Power Kids Press, 2015.

On the Internet

Chippewa Indian Facts from Northeast American Indian Facts https://native-american-indian-facts.com/Northeast-American-Indian-Facts/Chippewa-Indians-Facts.shtml

Ojibway Indian Fact Sheet from Native Languages of the Americas http://www.bigorrin.org/chippewa_kids.htm

The Ojibwa from Mr. Donn https://nativeamericans.mrdonn.org/northeast/ojibwa.html

Glossary

ally (AL-eye)—A friend.
bilingual (by-LING-wul)—Knowing how to speak two languages.
cradleboard (KRAY-dul-bord)—A wooden board to which babies could be fastened with blankets and carried on someone's back or set down for a nap.
embroider (em-BROY-der)—To decorate with a design of colorful stitches.
enmity (EN-mih-tee)—Hostility or ill will.
fast—To go without food for a long period of time.
hide—Animal skin.
mussel (MUS-ul)—A two-shelled sea organism that is harvested for food.
nettle (NEH-tul)—A plant with stinging leaves.
petticoat (PEH-tee-koht)—A thick slip or under skirt.
pharmacist (FAR-muh-sist)—An expert who is licensed to sell people medicine.
psychiatrist (sy-KY-uh-trist)—An expert who helps people with emotional or mental conditions.
sap—The liquid found in certain kinds of trees and plants.
scalp lock (SKALP-lok)—A long lock of hair grown on an otherwise shaved head.
shaman (SHAH-min)—A priest or holy person.
sinew (SIH-noo)—A piece of tough tissue such as a tendon or ligament, often removed from game to use as strong thread or rope.
superstition (soo-per-STIH-shun)—A belief based on magic or luck.
toboggan (tuh-BAH-gun)—A flat-bottomed wooden sled.
treaty (TREE-tee)—An agreement between two groups of people.
tunic (TOO-nik)—A long shirt.
vision quest (VIH-zun KWEST)—An attempt to have a dream of a guardian spirit, often through fasting.
wigwam (WIG-wahm)—A cone- or dome-shaped house.

INDEX

buffalo (bison) 6, 8, 29
Canada 12-13
canoes 18, 32, 35
Child, Brenda 27
Chippewa (Ojibwe)
    beliefs 8, 19, 36, 37-39, 40-42, 43
    children 4, 5-8, 39-40
    clans 9
    clothing 23-26, 41
    dream catchers 19
    food 28, 29-34
    language 18, 20, 21-23, 27
    moccasins 24-25
    names 8-9
    powwows 27, 41
    prayers 6, 11
    ricing 32, 35
    rules 5-7
    traditional lands 9-10, 13-15, 42
    treaties 16-17
    vision quests 8, 43

cradleboards 6
eagle 38, 39
European explorers 12, 13-15, 29
France 12-15
Grand Medicine Society 43
Gray, Gerald, Sr. 22
Indian Removal Act of 1830 17
maple syrup 33-34, 37
Pasey, Axel 43
reservations 10, 16, 17
rice 14, 32-33, 42
Rogers, John (Way-quah-gezhig) 7
shamans 39-40
snakeroot 7
Standing Rock 23
tepees 31
wars 13-14, 15
wigwams 4-5, 18, 30
wolf 39

PHOTO CREDITS: Cover, pp. 1, 2, 4, 6, 9, 15, 32, 33, 36, 40; p. 7—Homer Edward Price; p. 8—Jack Dykinga; p. 10—CJLippert; p. 11—Dept. of Agriculture; p. 12—Pinpin; pp. 14, 41—Maxpixel; p. 16—Jon Zander, Daderot; p. 17—Genericll39; p. 18—John B. Wilkinson; p.p. 31, 34—Pixabay; p. 20—Shandris; p. 22—Internet Archive Book Images; pp. 23, 25—Daderot; p. 24—Cliff; p. 26—Minnesota Historical Society; p. 27—Dept. of Interior; p. 28—Dimus; p. 30—F.A. MacDonald; p.35—Roland Reed; p. 38—Tony Hisgett; p. 39—Mark Kent; p. 42—WP Watchdog; p. 43—US National Archives. Every measure has been taken to find all copyright holders of material used in this book. In the event any mistakes or omissions have happened within, attempts to correct them will be made in future editions of the book.

MEET THE
AUTHOR

Tamra B. Orr is the author of hundreds of books for readers of all ages. She graduated with a degree in teaching from Ball State University in Indiana, and now lives in the beautiful Pacific Northwest with her family. When she isn't writing books, she is reading them. She loves researching and learning about history and the way people lived long ago. After learning about the Chippewa, she will never take rice or maple syrup for granted again.

2995

RECEIVED NOV 26 2019